Congressional
Research
Service

Natural Gas in the U.S. Economy: Opportunities for Growth

Robert Pirog
Specialist in Energy Economics

Michael Ratner
Specialist in Energy Policy

November 6, 2012

Congressional Research Service

7-5700

www.crs.gov

R42814

Summary

Due to the growth in natural gas production, primarily from shale gas, the United States is benefitting from some of the lowest prices for natural gas in the world and faces the question of how to best use this resource.

Different segments of the U.S. economy have different perspectives on the role natural gas can play. Suppliers, which have become the victims of their own production success, are facing low prices that are forecast to remain low. Some companies that have traditionally produced only natural gas have even turned their attention to oil in order to improve their financial situation. Smaller companies are having a difficult time continuing operations and larger companies, including international companies, have bought into many shale gas assets. Prices have remained low even as consumption has increased, in part, because producers have raised production to meet the demand and because companies have improved efficiency and extraction techniques. Some companies, many with large production operations, have applied for permits to export natural gas. This has raised concerns from consumers of natural gas that domestic prices will rise. The debate regarding exports is ongoing.

Industries that consume natural gas have seen input costs drop, and some have heralded low natural gas prices as the impetus for a manufacturing revolution in the United States. Some companies have begun to make major investments to take advantage of the low natural gas prices, particularly in petrochemicals. Other companies are waiting to see if prices will remain low long enough to warrant major investments in new facilities. Meanwhile, the electric power sector has already seen a transition from coal-fired generation to natural gas. Low natural gas prices are also putting pressure on renewable sources of power generation. However, increases in demand will put upward pressure on natural gas prices.

The transportation sector, the one part of the economy vulnerable to foreign energy supplies, is beginning to explore ways to use more natural gas. Transportation makes up less than 1% of U.S. natural gas consumption and would require billions of dollars in investment to increase that share significantly.

All of the change that has taken place so far has occurred despite environmental concerns and regulatory developments at the state and federal level that might curtail production. Natural gas is a fossil fuel that produces various pollutants, some more than other fossil fuels and some less. Methane, the major component of natural gas, is also a potent greenhouse gas when released without burning. Other environmental concerns focus on water use and disposal in hydraulic fracturing to extract natural gas from shale formations.

Over the next five years, many of the issues being debated now may be decided. The industry and market are adapting to the newly found supplies and the concerns associated with them, as well as integrating more natural gas into the economy. There are many evolving issues some of which Congress can influence directly because of statutes and some indirectly. On the demand side, legislation has been introduced regarding exports of liquefied natural gas and alternative fuels for vehicles. There has been other legislation related to environmental regulations of natural gas.

Contents

Figures

Tables

Appendixes

Contacts

Introduction: What To Do With All the Natural Gas?

The relatively rapid expansion of U.S. natural gas resources over the last five years, particularly from shale gas, has been coupled with slower demand growth by natural gas consumers. The result has been low prices not seen for over a decade and, equally important, prices that are projected to stay low for decades. U.S. natural gas prices have also been comparatively lower than those observed in international markets.

The projected persistence of rising supply and low prices has raised the question of how the United States will take advantage of its natural gas resources. Because of low prices, there have been requests by some producers to export natural gas in liquefied form (LNG), hoping to sell at higher world prices. Some consumer groups argue that exports will raise domestic prices, which will hurt businesses and households. Some businesses believe the low prices can spur a resurgence in U.S. manufacturing, particularly petrochemicals and other industries using large amounts of natural gas. Some environmentalists view natural gas as a key component for decreasing carbon dioxide (CO_2) emissions and other greenhouse gases, while other environmentalists believe that it is as polluting as coal, especially when derived from shale formations. Some analysts believe natural gas can enhance U.S. energy security if it can be used in transportation to replace gasoline. All these questions highlight the tremendous changes that have taken place in the U.S. energy landscape over the last few years and portend future changes.

There have been over 150 bills introduced in the 112th Congress that would affect both supply of natural gas (H.R. 840, S. 302, S. 706, and S. 1007, among others) and demand, with some targeting specific sectors such as LNG exports (H.R. 3913 and H.R. 4024, among others) and transportation (S. 734 and H.R. 970, among others). Legislation has also been introduced that would affect environmental issues associated with natural gas (H.R. 1084, H.R. 4322, and H.R. 6235, among others). This report examines what has changed in the natural gas industry and focuses on the demand side and ancillary benefits to the U.S. economy. This report does not address negative consequences to other economic sectors due to a shift to natural gas.

Background: The Market Has Changed

Shale Gas: The Game Changer

Without the development of shale gas, much of the discussion about integrating more natural gas into the economy would not be occurring. Over the last decade U.S. natural gas reserves have climbed tremendously, 72% since 2000 and 49% since 2005 (see **Figure 1**).[1] These data allow for reductions for natural gas produced during the period and so are "net" increases. In recent years, the increase in reserves is mostly attributed to development of shale gas, which has grown from 10% of U.S. natural gas reserves in 2007 to 32% in 2010. By comparison conventional U.S. natural gas reserves declined between 2007 and 2008, and fell again in 2010. Though the decline was marginal, it highlights the importance of shale gas to future U.S. natural gas production.

---

[1] Reserves is an industry term to define the likelihood that natural gas resources can be produced using current technology and at today's prices according to the Society of Petroleum Engineers and the World Petroleum Congresses definition.

Many industry analysts expect shale gas reserves to continue to rise and make up a greater portion of U.S. natural gas reserves unless new restrictions are placed on the industry, such as related to hydraulic fracturing, power plant emissions, etc.

Figure 1. U.S. Natural Gas Reserves and Production

2000 - 2010

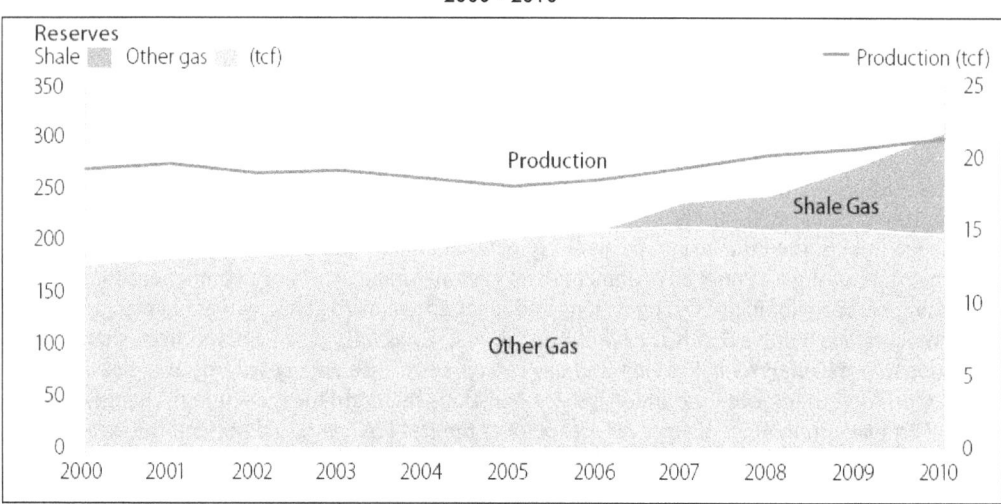

Source: U.S. Energy Information Administration—http://www.eia.gov/dnav/ng/
ng_enr_dry_a_EPG0_r11_bcf_a.htm, http://www.eia.gov/dnav/ng/ng_enr_shalegas_a_EPG0_R5301_Bcf_a.htm,
and http://www.eia.gov/dnav/ng/hist/n9070us2a.htm.

Notes: Although shale gas reserves existed prior to 2007, they were not as significant a portion of overall reserves and not tabulated prior to 2007. 2010 is the latest year data are available.

In 2011, the United States produced and consumed more natural gas than it ever has—23 trillion cubic feet (tcf) and 24 tcf, respectively—while paying some of the lowest market prices for natural gas in the world.[2] The production figure of 23 tcf is of dry gas, which has been processed for consumption purposes, but the United States actually produced 28.5 tcf of raw natural gas in 2011. The United States is the world's leading producer of natural gas, surpassing Russia in 2009, and the world's leading consumer. After declining for the first half of the last decade, U.S. natural gas production rose 18% in the latter half, with shale gas accounting for 25% of production by 2010.[3]

Reserves and production data do not tell the whole story when looking at the U.S. transformation regarding natural gas supply. The term *reserves* has a specific industry definition that includes a technological component, an economic factor, and a probability of success among other criteria. To more fully understand the changes to the U.S. natural gas sector it is more appropriate to look at reserves and estimates for undiscovered, technically recoverable resources (UTRR) (see **Figure 2**). UTRR is an estimate of what can be extracted using current technology regardless of price. Using UTRR plus reserves, the United States has a natural gas resource base of 1,809 tcf or enough gas for approximately 79 years of production at 2011 levels. Compared with data from

---

[2] Many producing countries subsidize natural gas consumption, so their consumers do not pay a market price.

[3] 2010 is the latest data is available for this metric.

2006, U.S. UTRR for natural gas has jumped almost 25%. Even this measure may not accurately reflect what will be extracted from the ground as technology is constantly changing. Just over the last few years, industry has been able to improve its shale gas extraction rate from about 5% to about 15%, thereby tripling what is recoverable.

Figure 2. Natural Gas Resources and Reserves

2006 vs. 2011

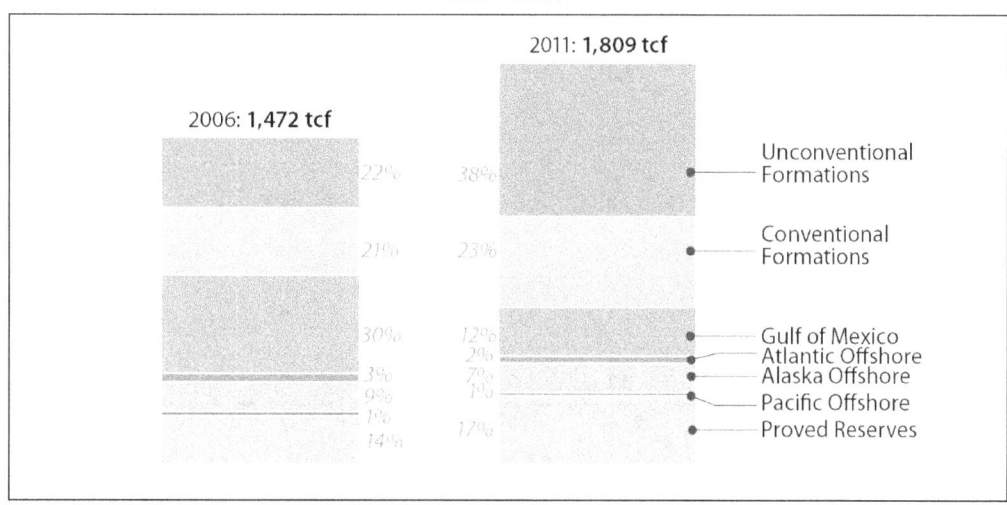

Source: Department of the Interior's U.S. Geological Survey and Bureau of Ocean Energy Management (BOEM) and U.S. Energy Information Administration.

Notes: The data for unconventional includes some but not all of the shale basins as some have not been assessed to date by the U.S. Geological Survey. Undiscovered technically recoverable resources (UTRR) refers to amounts of natural gas estimated to exist by examining geologic characteristics of unexplored areas and recoverable using current technology. All the figures in the graphic above are UTRR except Proved Reserves, which is defined as a 90% probability of recovery using existing technology and at current prices. Units = trillion cubic feet (tcf).

Projected Future Growth

In 2011, natural gas was the most produced fuel, on a tonne of oil equivalent basis, in the United States, surpassing coal for the first time. This change was driven by the success of shale gas development. The U.S. Energy Information Administration (EIA), which makes projections based on current policy and information, estimated in its *2012 Annual Energy Outlook* that overall U.S. natural gas production will grow 28% between 2010 and 2035 (see **Table 1**). Shale gas will comprise almost 49% of that production, up from 23% in 2010. During the time period the United States is expected to go from a net importer of natural gas by pipeline and LNG to a net exporter by 2022, which is a change from EIA's *2011 Annual Energy Outlook* when there was no time period in which the United States was forecast to be a net exporter of natural gas. The United States is forecast to be a net LNG exporter by 2016, according to EIA.

Table 1. U.S. Natural Gas Production Composition, Imports & Prices

Projections through 2035, tcf unless noted

	2010	2010 % of Total	2015	2020	2025	2030	2035	2035 % of Total
Associated Gas (Onshore)	1.4	6.5%	1.5	1.5	1.4	1.2	1.0	3.6%
Tight Gas	5.7	26.3%	6.1	6.1	6.2	6.1	6.1	21.9%
Shale Gas	**5.0**	**23.0%**	**8.2**	**9.7**	**11.3**	**12.4**	**13.6**	**48.9%**
Coalbed Methane	2.0	9.2%	1.8	1.8	1.8	1.7	1.8	6.5%
Other Non-Associated Gas	4.6	21.2%	3.8	3.4	3.0	2.7	2.4	8.6%
Lower 48 Offshore	2.6	12.0%	1.9	2.3	2.4	2.6	2.7	9.7%
Alaska	0.4	1.8%	0.3	0.3	0.3	0.3	0.2	0.7%
Total Production	21.7	100%	23.6	25.1	26.4	27.0	27.8	99.9%
Net Imports	2.6		1.7	0.4	(0.8)	(0.9)	(1.4)	
Spot Prices ($/MBtu)	$4.39		$4.29	$4.58	$5.63	$6.29	$7.37	

Source: EIA Annual Energy Outlook 2012, Reference Case, http://www.eia.gov/oiaf/aeo/tablebrowser/#release= AEO2012&subject=0-AEO2012&table=14-AEO2012&region=0-0&cases=ref2012-d020112c.

Notes: Data for 2010 are actual figures, but data going forward are projections by EIA under their Reference Case for the 2012 Annual Energy Outlook. Volume units = trillion cubic feet.

The only portion of U.S. production to significantly rise over the time period examined by EIA is shale gas. It grows both as a percent of overall production as well as in absolute terms. As a whole, conventional natural gas is estimated to make up a much smaller percent of the overall production mix, declining from 41.5% in 2010 to 22.7% in 2035. The decline of conventional natural gas sources demonstrates that natural gas is a finite resource, but how much may exist is still unknown.

Natural Gas Prices: A Competitive Advantage

A consequence of the rapid increase in natural gas supply is downward pressure on prices. U.S. spot natural gas prices, also known as the Henry Hub price or the NYMEX (New York Mercantile Exchange) price, are relatively low compared with domestic prices over the last decade as well as international prices over the last few years (see **Figure 3** and **Figure 5**).

Historically, natural gas prices in the United States have been volatile. From 1995 to 1999 the spot price of natural gas averaged $2.23 per MBtu, but increased to an average price of $4.68/MBtu during the 2000 to 2004 period, an almost 110% rise. From 2005 to 2009 the spot price averaged $7.23/MBtu hitting a peak of $15.38/MBtu in December 2005. Prices again spiked in July 2008. High prices, based on an assumption of a declining reserve base and production, seemed to indicate that the future would be characterized by much higher natural gas prices and domestic exposure to high-priced, imported LNG. However, prices started to decline in the latter half of 2008 because of the recession. As demand picked up in the 2010 to 2011 period, along with a warm winter, the average spot price of natural gas did not, declining to $4.20/MBtu. In the first eight months of 2012 spot prices averaged $2.55/MBtu.[4] These lower recent prices and optimistic expectations concerning domestic supply have led to a view that the United States will have plentiful supplies of natural gas available at low cost well into the future. Nevertheless, some industry participants have experienced price trends that reversed in the past and not all are ready to make financial commitments despite current low prices. As mentioned previously, shale gas production began coming to the market in 2007 and has been increasing ever since.

Figure 3. U.S. Natural Gas Prices

1990-2012

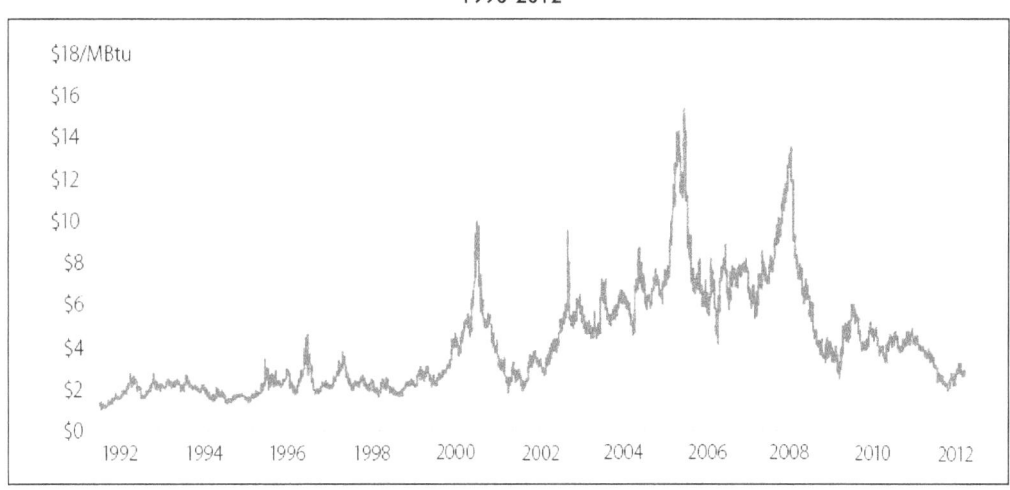

Source: Bloomberg New Energy Finance.

Notes: Units = dollars per million British thermal unit ($/MBtu).

The price of natural gas, as with other commodities, is driven by supply and demand. Demand for natural gas is affected by the economy, the weather, seasonality, product storage, and electrical use, among other factors (see **Figure 4**). The winter months in the United States are when demand for natural gas peaks, as it is used in residential and commercial buildings for heating. The United States also has a second, more modest peak, in the summer as more natural gas is consumed for electricity generation for air conditioning. This aspect of the demand cycle will vary depending upon the region of the country. During the months of approximately April through June, natural gas is normally produced and stored for the winter peak demand starting in November. As a consequence, storage plays a critical role in balancing the U.S. natural gas market and can greatly affect prices.

---

[4] Spot price data is from the Energy Information Administration, available at http://www.eia.gov/dnav/ng/ng_pri_fut_s1_d.htm.

Figure 4. Seasonal Natural Gas Demand

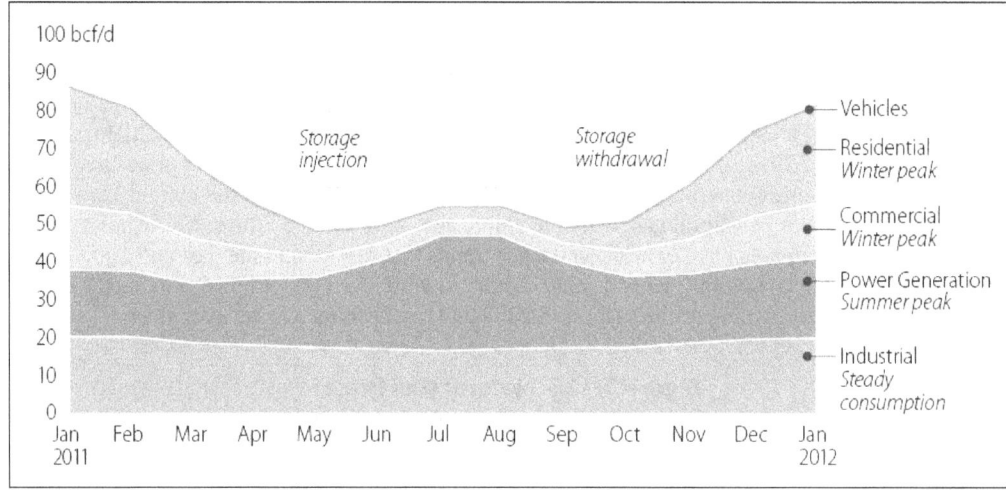

Source: U.S. Energy Information Administration (EIA) and Bloomberg New Energy Finance.

Notes: Units = billion cubic feet per day (bcf/d)

As an example, in Spring 2011 large underground storage facilities were being filled as typically happens, but the winter months later in the year were warmer than expected and storage levels remained high as less natural gas was used for heating. In the Spring of 2012, the high storage levels added additional downward pressure on prices, which dropped to about $2.00/MBtu for the first time since the 1990s. Producers of natural gas tend not to stop production from a well, unless prices are below their operating costs and they believe they will stay at that level for a long time, and even then companies may be hesitant to stop production. There are costs and technical issues involved with halting production, maintaining a well, and restarting production.

The advent of shale gas and the decline of U.S. natural gas prices has attracted global attention and prompted countries to try to emulate the U.S. success in developing their unconventional gas resources. Although other countries have touted their unconventional natural gas resources, no country has achieved the level of development of the United States, except Australia, in developing their coal seam gas. Canada is moving ahead with its shale gas development, but lags behind the United States. As can be seen in **Figure 5**, U.S. and other regional natural gas prices around the world moved in sync for most of the last decade even though there is not a global market for natural gas as there is with oil. From 2008 to 2009, natural gas prices dropped worldwide because of the decrease in demand from the decline in economic activity. U.S. shale gas was beginning to come to market in 2007/2008 and by 2010/2011 it changed the trajectory of U.S. natural gas prices from those of the rest of the world. In 2011, the rest of world faced higher prices than in 2010 for natural gas, but the United States saw its natural gas price decline by 9%. U.S. natural gas prices have continued to trend lower ever since, and many analysts forecast U.S. natural gas prices to remain relatively low at least through the end of this decade and possibly for longer.

Figure 5. Select Regional Natural Gas Prices

2001-2011

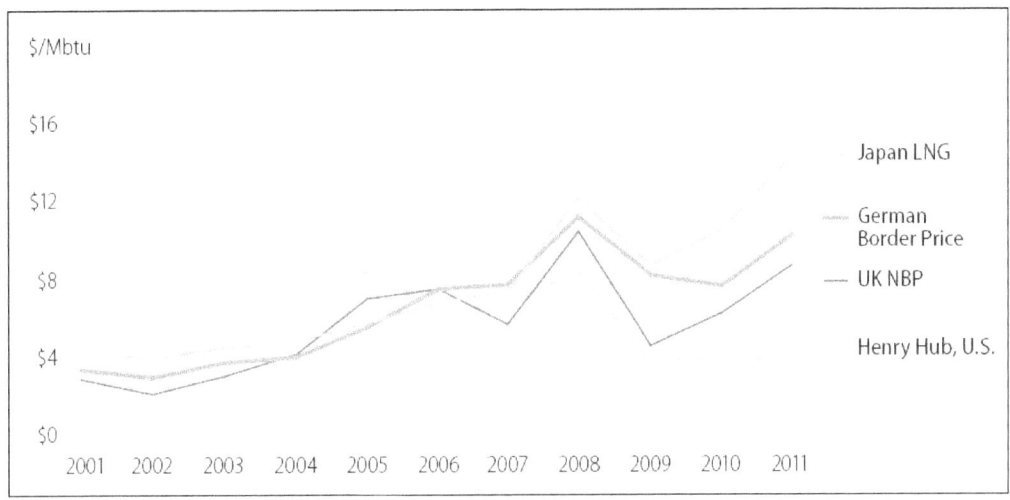

Source: BP Statistical Review of World Energy, 2012, June 2012, p. 27. http://www.bp.com/sectionbodycopy.do?categoryId=7500&contentId=7068481.

Notes: The German Border Price is a proxy for European oil indexed prices. Units = U.S. dollar per million British thermal units (MBtu).

The differential between the U.S. spot price and the average for the other major natural gas markets has been growing each year since 2007. Although there are many factors that can affect natural gas prices in a particular market for a certain period, such as the nuclear accident in Japan, the growing differential highlights how the U.S. natural gas market has been insulated from external events and the impact of the expanding U.S. natural gas resource base.

Contributing Factors

As natural gas prices in the United States have declined other market factors have begun to alter the industry and affect market fundamentals. In order to improve their revenues, many natural gas-oriented companies have added more oil-rich areas to their portfolios, particularly tight-oil formations, which have contributed to growing U.S. oil production.[5] However, with oil becoming the focus of production, natural gas infrastructure is not keeping pace and consequently natural gas is being flared in some areas of the United States in large quantities. Natural gas use displacing coal in electric generation has already shown the potential for decreasing emissions, as natural gas power generation releases about half the CO_2 of coal-fired generation. Additionally, companies are seeking further markets for natural gas and have applied for permits to export natural gas as LNG. As highlighted in **Figure 5**, the price for natural gas in the United States is lower than other major markets.

---

[5] For additional information on the shift to tight oil see CRS Report R42032, *The Bakken Formation: Leading Unconventional Oil Development*, by Michael Ratner et al.

Natural Gas Liquids: A Production Driver

Natural gas liquids (NGLs) have taken on a new prominence as shale gas production has increased and prices have fallen. NGL is a general term for all liquid products separated from natural gas at a gas processing plant and includes ethane, propane, butane, and pentanes. When NGLs are present with methane, which is the primary component of natural gas, the natural gas is referred to as either "hot" or "wet" gas. Once the NGLs are removed from the methane the natural gas is referred to as "dry" gas, which is what most consumers use. Each NGL has its own market and its own value. As the price for dry gas has dropped because of the increase in supply and other reasons such as the warm winter of 2011, the natural gas industry has turned its attention to producing more wet gas in order to bolster the value they receive. Some companies have shifted their production portfolios to tight oil formations, such as the Bakken in North Dakota, to capitalize on the experience they gained in shale gas development. Historically, the individual NGL products have been priced against oil, and as oil prices have remained higher since 2005 relative to natural gas, it has driven an increase of wet gas production, thereby maintaining the amount of dry gas as a production "byproduct" despite its low price.

Figure 6. Natural Gas, Oil, and NGL Prices

August 2008 to August 2012

Source: Bloomberg New Energy Finance.

Notes: The NGL blend prices are weighted to an average mix of 42% ethane, 29% propane, 11% normal butane, 6% iso-butane, and 13% natural gasoline and priced at Mont Belvieu, TX. The mix of NGLs will vary by source and the price will vary by the actual market for the product. The natural gas price is at Henry Hub and the oil price is West Texas Intermediate (WTI). August 2008 is when prices for all three commodities just started to decline from their peaks in July because of the recession. Units = million British thermal units (MBtu).

As can be seen in **Figure 6**, the price of natural gas at the end of August 2012 was approximately $3.20/MBtu, while the value of NGLs was almost $10.00/MBtu. The additional value that can be extracted above the price of natural gas is a driver of current production. Drilling rigs are being moved from dry gas fields to wet gas and predominantly oil fields, like the Bakken, that produce natural gas in association with oil production. The proportion and composition of NGLs varies by gas field and therefore the price differential will vary as well. The price differential between oil and NGLs is also diverging over the last year because the prices of ethane and propane, two main components of NGLs, are delinking from their historic connection to oil prices. As ethane and propane production has risen the last couple of years their prices have been driven more by their own market fundamentals of supply and demand.

Flaring: A Value Issue

As natural gas production began to increase in 2005, so did the amount of natural gas that was vented (released into the atmosphere) and flared (burned at the production site). Natural gas is either flared, which is preferred, or vented usually for safety or health reasons prior to connecting a well to a pipeline. This issue has grown in prominence as development of tight oil resources has increased because of the horizontal drilling and hydraulic fracturing techniques developed for shale gas has shifted to that sector. The Bakken formation has had the most notoriety because as its oil production has increased, so has the amount of natural gas that is being flared (over 20% of gross production in 2010).[6] Oil production in tight formations is expanding rapidly and the natural gas infrastructure to move the associated gas to market has lagged. The low price of natural gas has compounded the issue, particularly in jurisdictions that have relatively lax regulations when it comes to flaring.

Factors Affecting Production

The location of shale formations (see **Figure A-1**) has altered the movement of natural gas supplies to consuming markets in the United States. As an example, traditionally gas flowed from the Gulf Coast to the Northeast via large diameter, long-haul transmission pipelines. The discovery and production from the Marcellus Shale formation, which underlies much of West Virginia and Pennsylvania, southern New York, eastern Ohio, western Maryland, and western Virginia, has changed the need for gas from the Gulf Coast as the Marcellus is much closer to Northeast markets.[7] The reconfiguration of supply centers and consuming markets requires new infrastructure to be put in place, including gathering pipelines (small diameter pipelines that bring gas from the field to processing facilities), transmission pipelines, and processing facilities (plants that remove other hydrocarbons, i.e., NGLs, carbon dioxide, water, and nitrogen among other things before transmission and consumption). Additionally, other transmission pipelines will be reversed in order to bring the natural gas to different locations. This reconfiguration is an ongoing process that may cost the industry billions of dollars to achieve greater efficiencies.

Water is a key component of energy production, particularly for shale gas development that requires significant quantities for hydraulic fracturing.[8] Unfortunately, there are significant data gaps in this area that make evaluating the water needs of the energy sector difficult. A fracture treatment for a single zone may use more than 500,000 gallons of water.[9] Wells that need multiple treatments usually require between 3 million to 5 million gallons or more. For comparison, an

---

[6] U.S. Energy Information Administration, *Natural Gas Gross Withdrawals and Production*, database, 2010, http://www.eia.gov/dnav/ng/ng_prod_sum_dcu_snd_a.htm.

[7] For additional information on the Marcellus Shale Formation, see CRS Report R42333, *Marcellus Shale Gas: Development Potential and Water Management Issues and Laws*, by Mary Tiemann et al.

[8] For additional information on the role of water in natural gas production, see CRS Report R41507, *Energy's Water Demand: Trends, Vulnerabilities, and Management*, by Nicole T. Carter and CRS Report R42333, *Marcellus Shale Gas: Development Potential and Water Management Issues and Laws*, by Mary Tiemann et al.

[9] Department of Energy, Office of Fossil Energy and the National Energy Technology Laboratory, *Modern Shale Gas Development in the United States: A Primer*, DE-FG26-04NT15455, April 2009, pp. 58-59, http://fossil.energy.gov/programs/oilgas/publications/naturalgas_general/Shale_Gas_Primer_2009.pdf.

Olympic-size swimming pool holds over 660,000 gallons of water and the average daily per capita consumption of fresh water (roughly 1,430 gallons per day) works out to 522,000 gallons over one year.[10]

Historical Natural Gas Use

The transition to using more natural gas in the economy is already underway. Natural gas comprised 28% of the U.S. primary energy mix in 2011 and is on the upswing, while oil and coal have both declined in absolute terms and as a percent of consumption over the last decade. Historically, natural gas is well below its primary energy market share high of 34% in 1971, but just above its 20-year average of 26% (see **Figure 7**).

Figure 7. U.S. Primary Energy Consumption

1990-2011

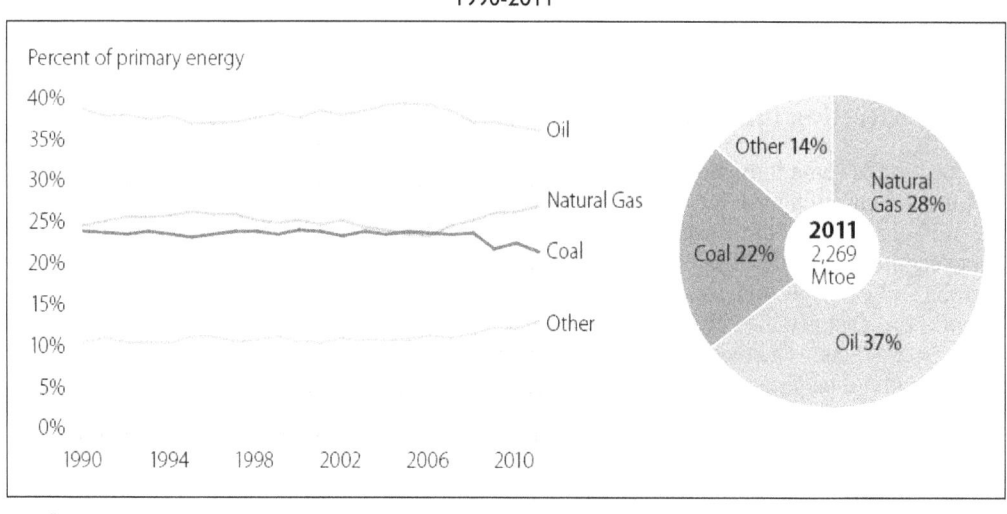

Source: BP Statistical Review of World Energy, 2012, June 2012. http://www.bp.com/ sectiongenericarticle800.do?categoryId=9037130&contentId=7068669.

Notes: Other primary energy includes nuclear, hydroelectricity and renewables. Units = million tonnes of oil equivalent (Mtoe).

Natural gas consumption, which is in part tied to economic activity, is on the rise in the United States after declining in 2009 because of the recession. Unlike oil, which is mostly consumed in transportation, and coal, which is mostly consumed in electricity generation, natural gas has more diversity to its consumption. Almost a third each of natural gas consumption is from electricity generation, industrial, and residential/commercial, which tends to use it similarly (see **Figure 8**). EIA divides consumption into five economic categories—residential, commercial, industrial, electric power, and transportation (vehicle fuel)—and two operational categories, lease and plant fuel (gas used for production and at processing plants) and pipeline and distribution use (gas used for compressors and to move gas to consumers). The two operational categories are usually not included when discussing U.S. gas consumption.

---

[10] U.S. Geological Survey, *Summary of Water Use in the United States, 2000*, http://ga.water.usgs.gov/edu/ wateruse2000.html.

Figure 8. U.S. Natural Gas Consumption by Sector
2001-2011

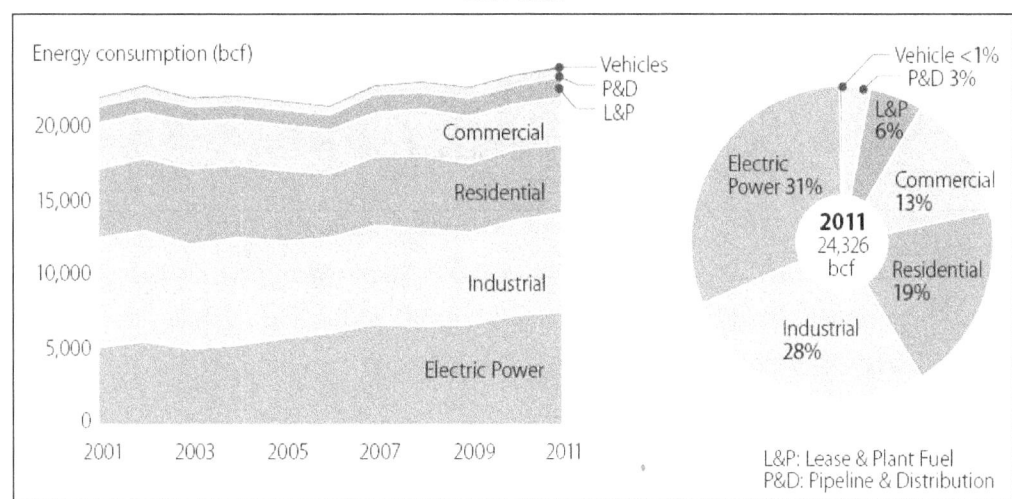

Source: U.S. Energy Information Administration, http://www.eia.gov/dnav/ng/ng_cons_sum_dcu_nus_a.htm.

Notes: Units = billion cubic feet (bcf).

All sectors increased in 2011 over 2010 figures, except residential consumption, which decreased, mainly due to warmer weather. There is limited additional residential and commercial use of natural gas unless new regional markets can be opened, which will require investment and infrastructure. Electric power generation makes up the biggest component of U.S. natural gas consumption followed by industrial use. (See sections "Electric Power Generation: First Mover" and "Petrochemicals: A Possible Rejuvenation.") However, the two sectors have essentially reversed position over the last decade, with electric power growing by about 10% since 2001 and industrial consumption declining by almost the same amount.

The reversal of the electric power and industrial sectors can be attributed to rising prices early in the decade that decreased industrial use and prompted much of the sector to move overseas. Electric generation from natural gas also decreased during the early part of the decade, but when prices started to decline because of the lower demand and then increased supply, natural gas-fired generation was the beneficiary. Some of the industrial sector is poised to return to the United States from overseas because of projected low natural gas prices, although in many cases companies are waiting to determine if low U.S. natural gas prices are sustainable.

In April 2012, for the first time in history, the amount of electricity generation from natural gas equaled that of coal, according to EIA statistics, each with about 32% of the market.[11] As mentioned above, natural gas use in electric generation has been growing over the previous decade, and will likely continue to grow, particularly if natural gas prices remain low. In addition, concerns about more stringent environmental regulations have in some cases contributed to the increase in retirement of coal-fired electricity generation, which largely is base-load capacity and is being replaced by natural gas generation.

---

[11] U.S. Energy Information Administration, *Net Generation by Energy Source: Total (All Sectors), 2002-June 2012*, July 2012, http://www.eia.gov/electricity/monthly/epm_table_grapher.cfm?t=epmt_1_1.

An apparent consequence of the shift to more natural gas-fired electric power generation in the first quarter of 2012 has been a decrease of U.S. carbon dioxide emissions by almost 8% to their lowest levels since 1992.[12] Besides more natural gas-fired electric power, EIA attributes the decline in emissions to reduced household heating because of the mild winter and reduced gasoline demand.

Figure 9. U.S. Natural Gas and Coal Prices

2008-2012

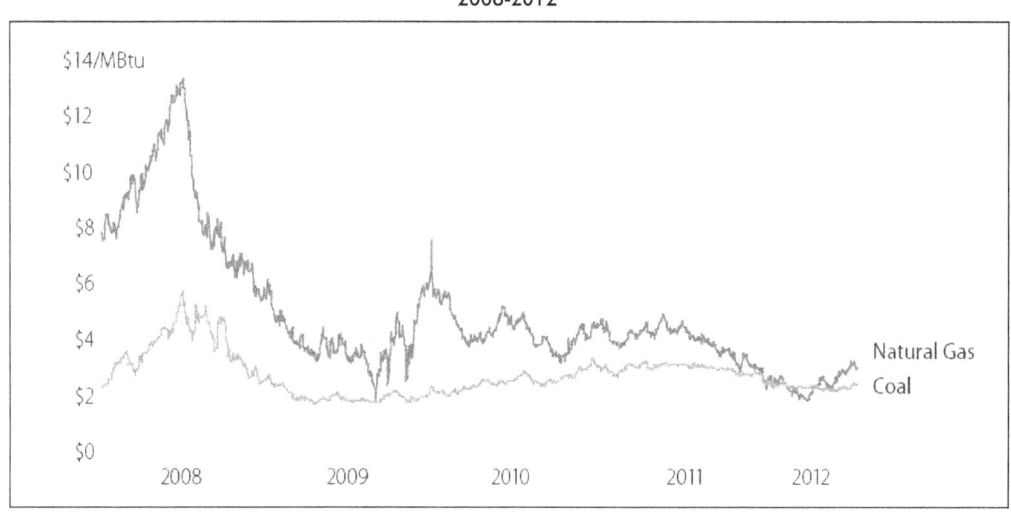

Source: Bloomberg New Energy Finance.

Notes: Units = dollars per million British thermal unit ($/MBtu).

Figure 9 also highlights the relative price variability of each commodity, with natural gas showing a much wider range than coal during the time period, as well as a significant decrease in the spread between natural gas and coal prices.

If large parts of the U.S. economy are to shift to natural gas, sufficiently low long-term prices that maintain the advantage of gas over other fuels are likely to be required. However, the increases in demand associated with these sectoral shifts in favor of gas use could result in prices also increasing, perhaps bringing into question the economic advantages available to potential users of natural gas. Further, if prices were to remain low in the long-term, industry might not be able to sustain production. If wellhead prices are too low for developers to make sufficient profits, exploration and development activities might slow and production might be capped. Market forces will likely establish a workable balance between the demand and supply sides of the market.

---

[12] U.S. Energy Information Administration, *U.S. Energy-Related CO2 Emissions in Early 2012 Lowest Since 1992*, August 1, 2012, http://www.eia.gov/todayinenergy/detail.cfm?id=7350.

Natural Gas Markets: The Possibilities

If natural gas were able to replace oil and coal in the fuel mix, it would require almost 77 tcf of natural gas per year; approximately tripling current U.S. consumption and production (see **Figure 10**). At that rate, even the current estimated resource base of 1,809 tcf would be exhausted in about 23 years. The amount of investment that would be required to undertake this change would be enormous, probably in the trillions of dollars, and new technologies and infrastructure would be needed to make the changes economical and practical, particularly in the transportation sector for natural gas vehicles.

Figure 10. 2011 Hydrocarbon Disposition

Natural gas requirements by sector

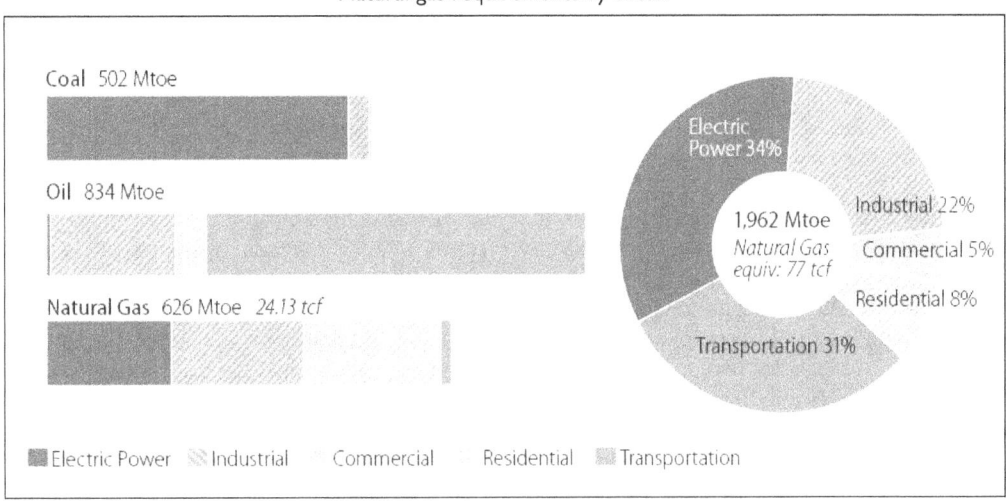

Data Source: BP Statistical Review of World Energy, 2012, and the U.S. Energy Information Administration.

Notes: Units = million tonnes of oil equivalent (Mtoe), which equates to 39.2 billion cubic feet.

Almost 24 tcf of natural gas would be required in the transportation sector alone, which is approximately the amount the United States consumed in total in 2011. Less than 1% of U.S. natural gas was consumed in the transportation sector in 2011. Although this scenario is beyond what could be achieved realistically, it highlights the central questions of this report as to how much natural gas the United States can produce and what sectors of the economy can use it.

Demand Response: Direct Beneficiaries

Expanded supply, coupled with low natural gas prices, has the potential to contribute to a transformation of important sectors of the U.S. economy. Increased output and employment, expanded investment, income growth, improved competitiveness, and a reduction in the foreign trade deficit are likely outcomes. These conditions in the natural gas markets are likely to benefit certain key industries directly, while many other industries could experience indirect benefits. Direct beneficiaries are those industries that use natural gas as a raw material or as an important input in a production process. Industries whose output is directly related to the expansion of natural gas exploration, development and production are also direct beneficiaries. Examples of industries that use natural gas directly are petrochemicals and fertilizers. The steel industry is an example of an industry whose output is linked to the pace of natural gas resource development. Industries experiencing indirect benefits might include construction and capital goods producers that contribute to the supply chain for the investment projects undertaken by expanding natural gas consumers. In addition, more spending by workers in all of these industries could increase the growth of a wide variety of consumer goods and retail firms. The economic benefits of shale gas development and production will also open areas not recently accustomed to natural gas production, for example, the Marcellus field in parts of Pennsylvania, Ohio, West Virginia, Maryland, Virginia, and New York.

In the international economy, those U.S. industries directly affected by expanded supply and low natural gas prices are likely to experience a competitive advantage over the producers of similar goods in other countries, resulting in increased exports from, and decreased imports to the United States. These effects would likely improve the U.S. trade deficit position. This advantage is likely to be maintained over time if the U.S. price of natural gas remains below those observed in other world regional markets (see **Figure 5**).[13] U.S. industry's advantage could be reduced through a process of world natural gas price convergence, especially in the three leading regional markets. However, for this to occur, traditional long-run contract terms, specifically linking natural gas prices to oil prices, would need to be changed to a more market-oriented method.

While low natural gas prices are likely to benefit many consuming industries, they have a depressing effect on the natural gas industry itself. If prices fall, and remain below critical levels, the industry could respond by reducing exploration and development activity, and/or capping existing wells. Although some of this has occurred, overall natural gas production continues to trend upwards, in part because of cost-reducing efficiency gains, and in part because of contract provisions.[14] Actions that reduce current and future supplies tend to cause the price of gas to rise. One mitigating factor to this price process is the extraction of natural gas liquids (NGLs) from wells (see "Natural Gas Liquids: A Production Driver"). These liquids are typically of high value and may validate the production of natural gas even in a low price environment for the natural gas itself, which assumes oil prices remain high. Also, for some industries, the ratio of the price of oil to the price of natural gas is more important to U.S. competitiveness than the absolute price of domestic natural gas. An example is petrochemicals, where U.S. producers use natural gas liquids as a feedstock for ethylene production while European producers tend to use naphtha, derived from crude oil. Increased production of ethane from shale gas development has given the U.S. petrochemicals industry a price advantage.

Electric Power Generation: First Mover[15]

As discussed earlier in this report, natural gas is expected to increase its share of electricity generating capacity. The broad reasons for this increase begin with the expected increases in

---

[13] There are three major regional natural gas markets; North America, Europe, and Asia. There is no recognized world price of natural gas comparable to that of crude oil. Historically, natural gas markets have been characterized by long-term contracts indexed to the price of oil, rather than demand and supply conditions. There is limited international trade in natural gas, likely insufficient to cause prices to converge in the regional markets.

[14] Clifford Krauss and Eric Lipton, "After the Natural Gas Boom," *New York Times*, Sunday Business, October 21, 2012.

[15] This section draws upon IHS Global Insight, "The Economic and Employment Contributions of Shale Gas in the United States," December 2011.

natural gas supply, along with low prices. Also important are the relatively lower carbon emissions of gas-fired plants relative to coal-fired power plants, and the relatively high capital investment costs of coal-fired plants compared to natural gas-fired plants.[16] An additional benefit for the power-generating industry related to natural gas-fired plants is flexibility. Natural gas facilities can increase or decrease generation much more efficiently and cheaply than coal-fired plants. Much of the increase in natural gas-fired generation has been from facilities that have been operating below capacity. Lower fuel costs have given these facilities an advantage over other generators.

As a result of these advantages natural gas-fired plants are expected to account for about 60% of new generating capacity in the United States between 2011 and 2035.[17] Job creation as a result of this shift to natural gas is likely to be small. Although construction and capital equipment jobs will be created as natural gas-fired power plants are constructed, these jobs are not permanent. The net number of jobs in electric power generating facilities is likely to be low because jobs in coal fired-plants may be lost as new gas-fueled plants begin operating. In addition, a reduced demand for coal from the electric power generating sector may result in mining jobs shrinking, while gas drilling jobs go up.

Coal will, however, retain an important share of the electric power market. Some large facilities have scrubbing equipment in place to reduce emissions and many large producers are located near coal mines, which insures low transportation costs. In contrast, in many cases new natural gas pipelines would have to be constructed to allow switching from coal to natural gas.[18] Additionally, should natural gas prices rise because of increased demand in electricity or other sectors, coal-fired generation will become more competitive again.

The expansion of natural gas as a fuel for electricity generation is expected to have important macroeconomic effects, even though direct job creation is not likely to be great. The reason for this is based on the cost structure of electric power generation, where fuel costs account for approximately 40% of total production costs. If the cost savings relative to natural gas use materialize, and if they are passed on to consumers in the form of lower electricity rates, household disposable income would increase. This increase could be used by households to finance the purchase of a wide variety of consumer goods. Commercial natural gas consumers could reap higher profits, or contain growth in the cost of goods sold, due to lower electricity costs. Industrial demand could experience similar benefits; however, the effects are likely to be less important as the percentage of total costs accounted for by electricity costs falls. The exception is the petrochemicals industry, where natural gas costs are a large part of total costs.

---

[16] As noted in the report, natural gas is already displacing coal in electric power generation, and retirement of older coal-fired generation has been announced. Natural gas emits less pollutants than coal when combusted, see **Table 2**, on a fuel comparison basis. When factoring in the efficiency of natural gas power plants compared with the coal facilities being retired, the emissions improvements are even greater.

[17] U.S. Energy Information Administration, *Annual Energy Outlook 2012*, June 25, 2012, http://www.eia.gov/forecasts/ aeo/sector_electric_power_all.cfm#powergen.

[18] For additional information on natural gas displacing coal in electric power generation, see CRS Report R41027, *Displacing Coal with Generation from Existing Natural Gas-Fired Power Plants*, by Stan Mark Kaplan. Please note that Mr. Kaplan is no longer with CRS, and questions can be referred to Richard Campbell with CRS.

Petrochemicals: A Possible Rejuvenation

Natural gas is used in the chemicals industry both as a fuel and as a raw material. As stated previously, when natural gas is produced it is mainly methane, but also may include NGLs. One NGL is ethane, which is used to produce ethylene. Ethylene, a key component in plastics, in turn, is used to produce a wide variety of consumer goods, ranging from food packaging to home siding and window frames, automotive anti-freeze, clothing, tires, and bottles.

In 2012, a number of chemical companies announced plans to invest in new plant capacity, expand existing facilities, or re-open plants near shale gas supplies. In April 2012, Dow Chemical announced $4 billion in expansions and new investment in Texas. Shell Chemical announced plans for an ethane cracking unit costing between $2 billion and $4 billion, to be constructed in Pennsylvania near Marcellus Shale natural gas supplies. Chevron announced plans for a $1 billion investment at its Baytown facility in Texas. In addition, Phillips Chemical, Westlake Chemical, and others announced investment plans related to low-cost shale gas availability.[19]

Many of these investment plans, if they ultimately come to fruition, will result in new production capacity becoming available over the next five years. Multi-billion dollar investments with time lags of up to five years before they generate cash flow suggest that the companies believe that the United States is entering a period of sustained low natural gas prices and growing supply. Without supply growth, the increase in demand from these facilities would likely push prices up. The history of natural gas prices in the United States, as shown in **Figure 3** demonstrates that neither high, nor low, gas price stability has been evident in the market for long periods of time.

The American Chemistry Council conducted a study of the effects on the U.S. economy of a one-time $16.2 billion investment program, over several years, in petrochemical plant and equipment related to low-cost natural gas availability.[20] Their assumption was that this level of investment would increase ethane capacity in the United States by 25%.[21] Their analyses determined that 17,000 new, relatively high paying jobs would be created in the chemical industry, along with 395,000 jobs outside the chemical industry. Tax revenues generated as a result of the investment program would be about $4.4 billion annually for federal, state and local governments. Output of the U.S. chemicals industry could increase by $32.8 billion and a total of $132.4 billion in output would be generated by the economy as a whole. Studies of this type assume various economic and other conditions which, if they should change, would also change the result. While the specific forecast values of studies estimating economic effects are unlikely to be precisely correct over time, they may indicate potential and order of magnitude.

It has been reported that the global ethylene production balance between oil-based naphtha and natural gas-based ethane has been about 80:20 in favor of naphtha. However, the balance has tipped to 50:50, even before the large U.S. investments in ethane capacity have come on stream. This shift in input utilization has had negative effects on the international naphtha market, both for the U.S. and foreign markets. U.S. refiners report an excess of naphtha, much of which is

---

[19] Shauk, Zain, "Cheap Natural Gas Feeds Chemical Industry Boom," *Houston Chronicle*, April 19, 2012.

[20] "Shale Gas and New Petrochemicals Investment: Benefits for the Economy, Jobs, and U.S. Manufacturing," Economics and Statistics, American Chemistry Council, March 2011.

[21] There are some U.S. petrochemicals companies that use naphtha as a feedstock in their production, and many are believed to be shifting to NGLs. It does not appear that any possible negative consequences were factored into the American Chemistry Council study.

appearing in the European market, causing a supply glut and falling prices. European refiners, experiencing poor economics due to the euro crisis and the onset of recession, are suffering further losses due to the new competition from the United States. The normally high price of naphtha, comparable to that of gasoline, makes the competition more economically damaging for European refiners.[22]

The Fertilizer Industry Could Help Farmers

Natural gas is the primary raw material in nitrogen-based fertilizer production. From 70% to 90% of the estimated cost of producing nitrogen-based fertilizers is related to the cost of natural gas. In the 2000s, when natural gas prices for industrial consumers more than doubled, closure of ammonia plants, which supply the raw material for fertilizers, followed suit, rising from 13 in 2002 to 26 in 2007. While some of this capacity moved overseas, some was permanently closed. It would take time and investment to reinstate U.S. capacity. If U.S. fertilizer production could recover and pass on lower costs to farmers, this could lower the cost of food and ethanol for use in transportation, and have employment benefits in the fertilizer industry as well as those industries whose costs had decreased.

In the short-run few of these economic benefits can be observed. The fertilizer industry appears to be taking a wait-and-see attitude with respect to natural gas prices before major investment decisions in capacity expansion are undertaken. The industry, which suffered from high and volatile natural gas prices in the U.S. market, is likely to need compelling evidence that gas supplies will remain abundant and prices low in the future. For now, U.S. fertilizer cost savings due to low natural gas prices are balanced in favor of increased profits for producers compared to cost savings for consumers. This condition is encouraged by the rapidly increasing demand for corn which is keeping the demand for fertilizers high. For the period 2000 to 2006, the average acreage of planted corn in the United States was 79 million. In 2011 the total increased to 92 million, an increase of 16%, and the total is expected to continue rising.[23]

Steel Production: Two-Fold Winner

The expansion of shale gas and tight oil exploration and development has had an expansionary effect on the U.S. steel industry. Product demand has increased, while operating costs have declined. Natural gas exploration generates demand for tubular goods used for pipes, tubes, and joints in gas drilling equipment. In addition, natural gas is being substituted for coal as an input in the steel industry's blast furnaces, driving down costs per ton.[24]

Steel facilities located in, or near, areas of shale gas development are experiencing growth. For example, the steel industry in Ohio has been reported to be in the process of adding some two million feet of production space, costing $1.5 billion.[25] A number of companies, including Timken, United States Steel, Vallourec & Mannesmann, and a United States Steel-Kobe Steel

---

[22] Reuters, "U.S. Shale Gas Boom Brings Bad News for Europe's Oil Refiners," July 26, 2012.

[23] Simon Constable, "How Corn Is Feeding Fertilizer," available at http://barrons.com/article/SB50001424053111903835404577347881696361296.html, April 21, 2012.

[24] John W. Miller, "Steel Finds a Sweet Spot in the Shale," *Wall Street Journal*, March 26, 2012.

[25] Keith Schneider, "As Demand Rises, Ohio's Steel Mills Shake Off the Rust and Expand," *New York Times*, April 24, 2012.

joint venture project are located in Ohio in Canton, Youngstown, Lorain, and Leipsic. Because steel is a capital intensive, mechanized industry these plants are expected to produce about 630 jobs.[26] Many more construction jobs have been created in conjunction with these investment projects. As shale gas development expands overseas, these companies plan to expand their exports of energy industry related steel components.

The steel demand tied to shale gas expansion is mostly associated with drilling and infrastructure development. These activities are primarily front-loaded, taking place early in the development of the resource base. The industry must balance meeting these relatively short-run demands against long-run capacity expansion requirements to avoid excess capacity in the future.

While shale gas driven increases in demand have been important to the steel industry, the large supplies of low cost natural gas have been of less direct importance to the industry. The primary cost category in steel production that is likely to be affected by cheap natural gas is electricity; however, electricity costs account for only about 10% of total production costs.[27] As a result, the cost reductions experienced by the steel industry are likely to be small. The primary cost in steel production is scrap steel which is unaffected by the cost of natural gas.

Transportation: Key to Energy Independence?

Concerns about U.S. energy security and energy independence revolve around the use of imported oil as the country is basically independent in all other forms of energy. The Obama Administration targeted a one-third reduction in oil imports from when the President took office or a 3.6 million barrel per day cut by the end of the decade.[28] While oil based products, gasoline and diesel fuel are the major fuels used in transportation, natural gas does not play a big role.[29] Although natural gas consumption by vehicles has grown by 38% from 2006 through 2011, it still represents less than 1% of U.S. natural gas consumption.[30] However, the low current and projected price of natural gas has the commercial truck industry, in particular, planning for ways to incorporate more natural gas into the transportation fuel mix. Even in EIA's most aggressive case for heavy duty vehicles running on natural gas, in 2035 natural gas comprises less than 9% of the highway vehicle fuel mix.[31]

Natural gas can become a greater part of the transportation fuel mix in a variety of ways: compressed natural gas (CNG), LNG, methanol, gas-to-liquids, fuel cells, and electricity. However, the primary near-term opportunities for natural gas in long-distance trucking are LNG and CNG. The use of natural gas as a transportation fuel in any form will require changes in the sector from consumers and suppliers. New vehicles will need to be developed on a large scale, in

---

[26] Ibid.

[27] IHS Global Insight, "The Economic and Employment Contributions of Shale Gas in the United States," December 2011.

[28] The White House, *Remarks by the President on America's Energy Security*, Washington, DC, March 30, 2011, http://www.whitehouse.gov/the-press-office/2011/03/30/remarks-president-americas-energy-security.

[29] For additional information on natural gas vehicles, see CRS Report RS22971, *Natural Gas Passenger Vehicles: Availability, Cost, and Performance*, by Brent D. Yacobucci.

[30] U.S. Energy Information Administration, http://www.eia.gov/dnav/ng/ng_cons_sum_dcu_nus_a.htm.

[31] Energy Information Administration, *Annual Energy Outlook*, DOE/EIA-0383(2012), June 24, 2012, http://www.eia.gov/forecasts/aeo/index.cfm.

some cases requiring new technologies; new infrastructure will need to be deployed; and investments will need to be made by both consumers and industry.

Some inroads are being made in the transportation sector and additional efforts are being undertaken. Fleet trucks, including Waste Management, United Parcel Service, and AT&T among others, appear to be trying to take advantage of low natural gas prices.[32] Trucks can either be purchased new that run on natural gas, or conversion kits can be used to allow trucks that currently run on diesel fuel to use natural gas. Some retrofit conversions allow trucks to run on either LNG or diesel, allowing owners to take advantage of changing prices. The market for fuels for trucking is large. Approximately 3.2 million big-rig trucks use about 25 billion gallons or 1.7 million barrels per day, about 9% of U.S. oil consumption, of diesel fuel annually.[33]

Among the key factors in natural gas as a transportation fuel is the price spread between diesel fuel and natural gas. The cost of diesel fuel largely depends on the cost of crude oil. Historically, a barrel of oil cost about six times the cost of a unit of natural gas. As the price of oil has increased and the price of natural gas has fallen, a barrel of oil might cost over 30 times the cost of a unit of natural gas. This price spread has resulted in a price of diesel fuel twice as high as CNG on a diesel-gallon-equivalent basis.[34] The importance of the price spread between crude oil and natural gas demonstrates that natural gas can lose its competitive advantage because of a price rise, but it can also be lost if the price of crude oil falls. If a switch to natural gas-powered trucks increased the demand for new trucks many industries would expand production including the steel, tire, electronic, and vehicle manufacturing industries.

Long-haul trucking has made some progress to use natural gas, but concerns over the availability of refueling stations remain a hurdle. Shell announced a plan to add LNG pumps at 100 locations owned by Travel Centers of America for truck refueling.[35] The goal would be for LNG trucks to be able to travel across the entire country. Currently, city buses and local delivery trucks that return to a central facility where re-fueling is available are the primary consumers of natural gas in transportation. In addition, these users of natural gas tend to have short, or predicable, routes so that refueling can be reliably planned.

Residential and Commercial Consumption: A Regional Opportunity

Overall residential use of natural gas is not projected to increase as significantly as other sectors of the economy, and according to EIA estimates, may decline by 2035.[36] New infrastructure, both for consumers and industry, would be required to open new market areas to natural gas, and the increase in demand would have to warrant the investment. Nevertheless, there are some parts of the country where it may make sense.

---

[32] Rebecca Smith, *Wall Street Journal*, online edition, "Will Truckers Ditch Diesel?", Business Section, May 23, 2012.

[33] Ibid.

[34] Ibid.

[35] Christopher Helman, "Shell Investing $300M To Fuel LNG-Powered Trucks," *Forbes*, June 13, 2012.

[36] U.S. Energy Information Administration, *Annual Energy Outlook 2012*, Washington, DC, June 2012, http://www.eia.gov/oiaf/aeo/tablebrowser/#release=AEO2012&subject=2-AEO2012&table=2-AEO2012&region=1-0&cases=ref2012-d020112c.

As an example, in April 2011, New York City passed regulations to phase out the use of certain heating oils by 2030, and to replace them by cleaner-burning fuels, including natural gas.[37] However, new infrastructure will be required to bring additional volumes of natural gas, which will require local and federal approval. In 2010, New York State consumed almost 30 million barrels of distillate, which is one type of heating oil used for residential and commercial heating—almost half of the state's total distillate use.[38] Additionally, the states in New England consumed almost 50 million barrels of distillate in residential and commercial use. Expanding the natural gas infrastructure in these areas could help consumers take advantage of low natural gas prices, particularly given the region's proximity to the Marcellus Shale formation. Connecticut is an example of a state whose natural gas use is constrained by a lack of natural gas infrastructure.[39] The state is developing a plan to increase its natural gas consumption.

Increased sales of natural gas appliances, although a relatively small consumer group, could foster a change in perception of natural gas use. Besides the traditional appliances of stoves and hot water heaters, other household items like air conditioners could run on natural gas instead of electricity. Greater use of natural gas in this area could better integrate natural gas in the economy. Programs, like the Energy Star ratings on appliances, may need to be examined for how natural gas appliances are evaluated compared to other fuels.

Imports and Exports: A Reversal of Roles

Exports of natural gas have been on the rise, while imports have been declining. Increased exports, particularly as LNG, could provide a new demand center for U.S. supplies. Heading into the last decade, the United States was expected to be a growing importer of natural gas because domestic production was declining and demand was rising. EIA, in its 1999 Annual Energy Outlook, projected that net natural gas imports would grow between 1997 and 2020 from 12.9% of consumption to 15.5%, based on consumption growing faster than production.[40] To accommodate the potential increase in imports, five new LNG import terminals were built by industry in the latter half of the 2000s and some existing facilities were re-commissioned and expanded. The United States currently has LNG import capacity of almost 14 billion cubic feet per day (bcf/d) or over five trillion cubic feet (tcf) per year. However, higher domestic production—mainly from shale gas development—has made imports less necessary and they have been trending down over the last five years (see **Figure 11**). Import terminals are operating well below capacity. In its 2012 Annual Energy Outlook, EIA forecasts the United States becoming an overall net exporter of natural gas in 2022 and a net LNG exporter by 2016.

---

[37] Bill Holland, "Bloomberg Doubles Down on Natural Gas for New York City," *Platts*, August 28, 2012, online edition.

[38] U.S. Energy Information Administration, *Sales of Distillate Fuel Oil by End Use*, http://www.eia.gov/dnav/pet/pet_cons_821dst_dcu_nus_a.htm.

[39] John Kemp, "Connecticut Contemplates Connecting More To Gas Network," *ThompsonReuters*, October 19, 2012, online edition.

[40] U.S. Energy Information Administration (EIA), *Annual Energy Outlook 1999 with Projections to 2020*, DOE/EIA-0383(99), Washington, DC, December 1998, p. 71, http://www.eia.gov/oiaf/archive/aeo99/pdf/0383(99).pdf.

Figure 11. U.S. Imports and Exports

2007-2012

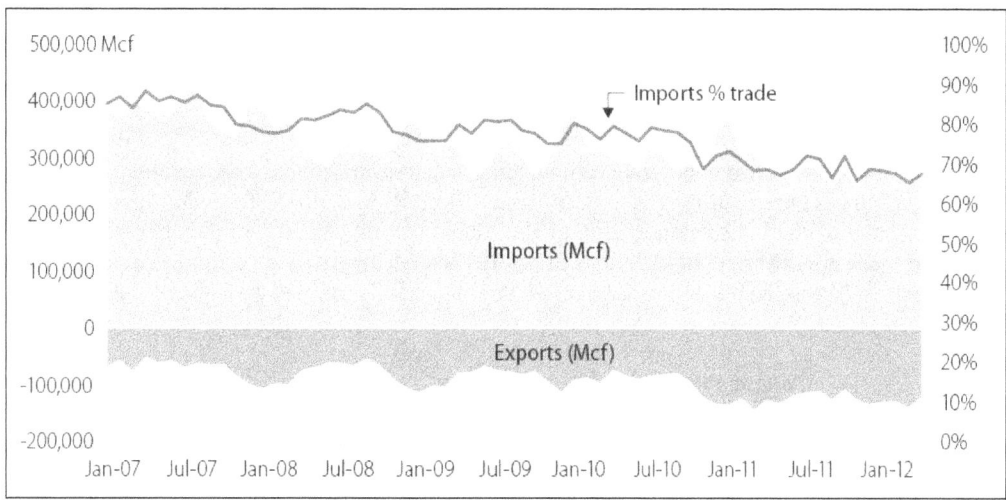

Source: U.S. Energy Information Administration.

Notes: Units = million cubic feet (Mcf).

The abundance of new domestic natural gas supplies is shifting industry interest from building LNG import terminals to constructing LNG export terminals.[41] As of September 2012, 18 companies had applied for permits to construct liquefaction facilities at existing LNG import terminals or build new facilities, with a capacity of 27.4 bcf/d or 10.0 tcf per year.[42] Increased pipeline exports to Canada[43] and Mexico may also rise if those countries' domestic production continues to decline and their demand continues to increase. It is unclear if, when, and how much LNG exports will be allowed, but the effect on domestic prices is at the crux of the debate. Any exports would be an additional source of demand and would likely put upward pressure on prices.

Other Sectors That Could Gain

How natural gas ultimately filters through the economy and what other sectors may benefit is not clear at this point in time and there are many other industries that stand to benefit that have not been addressed in this report. The oil industry has probably been the biggest indirect beneficiary of shale gas development and low natural gas prices. Production companies have used the same techniques—directional drilling and hydraulic fracturing—to unlock tight oil formations and increase U.S. oil production. Also, the petroleum refining sector should gain as natural gas is used as a fuel and feedstock. The airline industry has tested synthetic aviation fuels derived from natural gas. In 2009, Qatar Airways flew the first commercial flight using a natural gas-based jet

---

[41] For additional information on U.S. natural gas exports, see CRS Report R42074, *U.S. Natural Gas Exports: New Opportunities, Uncertain Outcomes*, by Michael Ratner, Paul W. Parfomak, and Linda Luther.

[42] Department of Energy, Office of Fossil Energy, *Summary of LNG Export Applications*, Washington, DC, September 21, 2012, http://fossil.energy.gov/programs/gasregulation/reports/Long_Term_LNG_Export_Table_08_17_12.pdf.

[43] For additional information on the U.S.-Canada energy relationship see CRS Report R41875, *The U.S.-Canada Energy Relationship: Joined at the Well*, by Paul W. Parfomak and Michael Ratner.

fuel.[44] The shipping industry is analyzing whether natural gas can be used as a bunker fuel. The paper and aluminum industries, which use large quantities of natural gas, may benefit. The aluminum industry has announced a couple of expansions and greenfield projects.

Natural Gas Markets: The Limitations

Market forces in conjunction with a dynamic regulatory environment have the potential to raise the role natural gas contributes to the U.S. economy. Optimistic outlooks for rising supply and low prices have sparked interest in expanding the role of natural gas even further. Congress has expressed interest in a variety of the issues of this debate. Members and committees have introduced legislation, held hearings, and offered opinions and inquiries with government agencies.

Many producers and consumers of natural gas seem confident that abundant supplies of natural gas will be produced regardless of the risks still outstanding. Some companies on both the supply and demand side of natural gas have made, or have announced plans for large investments to confirm their positions. Other companies are waiting to see how various dimensions of the debate unfold. A key component of this discussion is how domestic prices will react under different market conditions. As demand rises so does the pressure on prices to rise, which signals more production is needed, or that consumption should be curtailed. The beneficial economic effects of expanded natural gas supplies are not pre-ordained. Market and regulatory factors could come into play, having the effect of reducing positive economic benefits for the United States.

The Global Market: A Role for the United States

The prospect of increasing U.S. LNG exports has become encumbered by concerns of higher domestic prices and increased volatility of prices. As required by the Energy Policy Act of 2005, the Department of Energy (DOE) must issue a permit to export natural gas to countries with which the United States does not have a free trade agreement (FTA).[45] DOE must also determine that export to non-FTA countries is in the public interest. As part of that determination DOE has undertaken a two-part study to examine the impact of LNG exports on domestic prices, which is expected to be completed in early 2013. It is not anticipated that any additional permits for export to non-FTA countries will be approved before part two is completed, and outside of South Korea, the FTA countries do not import a significant amount of LNG.

Exports of energy-related resources have not been a big part of U.S. trade so increasing them would likely improve the overall U.S. trade balance. Nevertheless, the rise in U.S. natural gas production has already benefitted the U.S. trade position by dramatically decreasing imports, the other component of the trade balance. Increasing U.S. LNG exports would also expand the role of the United States in international natural gas markets. Asian countries, in particular, and some European countries have called for more U.S. LNG exports.

---

[44] Adam Schreck, "Qatar First to Fly with Jet Fuel Based on Natural Gas," *Associated Press*, October 13, 2009, online edition.

[45] Free Trade Agreement countries that require national treatment include Australia, Bahrain, Canada, Chile, Costa Rica, Dominican Republic, El Salvador, Guatemala, Honduras, Jordan, Mexico, Morocco, Nicaragua, Oman, Peru, Singapore, and South Korea.

If all the proposed LNG exports came to fruition, which is unlikely, the United States could become the world's largest LNG exporter. The United States is already the largest producer and consumer of natural gas and has the most storage capacity of any country in the world. These factors, coupled with proposed construction of LNG export terminals on the East Coast, Gulf Coast, and West Coast, could propel the United States into the center of the global natural gas trade, benefiting the U.S. balance of trade.

Unlike some other countries, where the government controls natural resources, the private sector controls U.S. natural gas resources and is driven mostly by market forces. However, becoming a significant global supplier could enhance certain U.S. national security priorities, such as contributing to European natural gas supply diversification from Russia and providing a counter to the nascent gas cartel, the Gas Exporting Countries Forum, which includes Russia and Iran.[46] Other effects beyond national security could include market and price reforms, technology transfers, greater transparency, and environmental benefits.

The domestic situation may also have an effect on the rest of the world as major U.S. companies with large international portfolios, in particular, continue to buy into shale gas assets. These companies are becoming more natural gas oriented. Many have already started looking for opportunities to use the experience they have gained in the United States in other countries. Additionally, many foreign companies have bought into U.S. shale gas areas to gain experience in producing these formations and eventually bring the technology back to their respective countries.

Before the expansion of U.S. LNG exports occurs, a decision is likely to be made concerning whether energy security means relying primarily on captive domestic, or regional, supplies, or whether it means participating in a well-supplied, open world market. A large expansion of LNG exports means that the domestic demand for natural gas will increase. If that extra demand is not met with additional supply increases, prices are likely to rise. If prices rise, the economic advantage of U.S. LNG will diminish somewhat. Additionally, the natural gas consuming industries that forecasted low prices and, as a result, increased their capital investment will likely not experience returns that meet expectations. Consumers in all categories will likely face higher costs. If exports of LNG are not permitted, or permitted at a low rate, most of the potential foreign trade benefits outlined in this report may not materialize. Prices could, nevertheless, rise if production is curbed.

Environmental Considerations[47]

With the advent of shale gas development, natural gas has been touted as a bridge fuel to a low carbon, renewable energy-based economy. Natural gas is cleaner burning than its hydrocarbon rivals—emitting less CO_2, particulate matter, sulfur dioxide, and nitrogen oxides, on average, than either coal or oil (see **Table 2**). But the use of new technologies and drilling practices, as well as the gas drilling boom they have engendered, has led to other environmental concerns and controversies. These concerns centered initially on water quality issues, including the substantial use of water during hydraulic fracturing activities as well as the potential contamination of water

---

[46] For additional information on European energy security, see CRS Report R42405, *Europe's Energy Security: Options and Challenges to Natural Gas Supply Diversification*, coordinated by Michael Ratner.

[47] Research by Mary Tiemann and Richard Lattanzio contributed to this section.

by hydraulic fracturing chemicals and wastewater disposal. Concerns have since incorporated other issues, such as land use changes, potential for induced seismicity from produced water injection, infrastructure requirements, and emissions of air pollutants from extraction operations and transport. The spectrum of concerns over hydraulic fracturing in unconventional reservoirs has led, in part, to various grassroots movements, some political opposition, and calls for regulatory actions and moratoria at the local, state, and federal levels.

Table 2. Air Pollution Emissions by Combusted Fuel Type

Pounds per Billion Btu of Energy Input

Pollutant	Natural Gas	Oil	Coal
Carbon Dioxide	117,000	164,000	208,000
Carbon Monoxide	40	33	208
Nitrogen Oxides	92	448	457
Sulfur Dioxide	1	1,122	2,591
Particulates	7	84	2,744
Formaldehyde	0.750	0.220	0.221
Mercury	0.000	0.007	0.016

Source: Energy Information Administration (EIA), Office of Oil and Gas. Carbon Monoxide: derived from EIA, *Emissions of Greenhouse Gases in the United States 1997,* Table B1, p. 106. Other Pollutants: derived from Environmental Protection Agency, *Compilation of Air Pollutant Emission Factors, Vol. 1, 1998.*

Notes: No pre- or post-combustion removal of pollutants. Bituminous coal burned in a spreader stoker is compared with No. 6 fuel oil burned in an oil-fired utility boiler and natural gas burned in an uncontrolled residential gas burner. Conversion factors are: bituminous coal at 12,027 Btu per pound and 1.64% sulfur content; and No. 6 fuel oil at 6.287 million Btu per barrel and 1.03% sulfur content—derived from Energy Information Administration, Cost and Quality of Fuels for Electric Utility Plants (1996). Coal specifications can vary greatly and each variety has a different emissions profile.

Major oil and gas producing states have been reviewing and revising their oil and gas rules in response to technological changes in the industry, and specifically to advances in hydraulic fracturing and directional drilling. Although oil and gas exploration and production is regulated primarily at the state level, several regulatory developments are occurring at the federal level as well.

The Environmental Protection Agency (EPA) has pursued initiatives related to hydraulic fracturing under three federal environmental statutes. In August 2012, EPA promulgated regulations under the authority of the Clean Air Act (CAA) that establish new air emissions standards for hydraulically fractured gas wells and other oil and gas production activities. The new rules entered into effect on October 15, 2012. Under the Safe Drinking Water Act (SDWA), EPA has issued draft Underground Injection Control (UIC) Program Guidance for Permitting Hydraulic Fracturing with Diesel Fuels.[48] This guidance is being developed in response to a provision of the Energy Policy Act of 2005 which revised the SDWA definition of underground injection to explicitly exclude the underground injection of fluids (other than diesel fuels) used in hydraulic fracturing operations. Final guidance is expected in Spring 2013. Under the Clean

---

[48] For additional information on the role of the Safe Drinking Water Act, see CRS Report R41760, *Hydraulic Fracturing and Safe Drinking Water Act Issues,* by Mary Tiemann and Adam Vann.

Water Act (CWA), EPA is developing regulations governing the discharge of wastewater produced in natural gas extraction from shale formations and coal beds. The regulations will be established under EPA's effluent guidelines program, which sets national standards for the discharge of pollutants from industrial activities directly to surface waters and municipal wastewater treatment facilities. EPA plans to propose regulations for the coalbed methane effluents in 2013, and for the shale gas extraction regarding wastewater pollutants in 2014.[49]

In May 2012, the Bureau of Land Management (BLM), Department of the Interior, proposed revisions to its oil and gas development rules in response to the increased use of hydraulic fracturing on federal and Indian lands. The proposal would require public disclosure of chemicals used during hydraulic fracturing, tighten requirements related to well-bore integrity, and add requirements for managing water used and produced in hydraulic fracturing operations. The public comment period closed September 10, 2012, and the BLM is now reviewing comments.

A tighter regulatory environment for natural gas exploration and production, if it raises costs significantly, would likely result in slower supply growth, and in the extreme could reduce some of the economic benefits described in this report. If demand increases as the result of expectations of rising supply and low prices, but then regulation slows supply growth, a price spike is the likely result. A price spike could reduce market confidence and set back the use of natural gas, especially in the industrial sector. Some companies in the industrial demand sector, as mentioned earlier, have made significant investments predicated on the supply being available and prices remaining low. However, in the past several years, a number of states have adopted stricter production regulations, yet production has continued to grow in those states (e.g., Colorado, North Dakota, Ohio, Pennsylvania, and Wyoming). In contrast, New York State essentially has a moratorium on high-volume hydraulic fracturing while regulations are revised. Overall, it is difficult to generalize regarding the potential effect of regulations. For example, EPA projects that the capture of natural gas required under its new air rules could have a net positive benefit for natural gas producers because of the value of the gas that could be saved and sold.

Price Levels and Volatility: Not a Certainty

The ability of U.S. industry to be positively affected by the evolving position of the United States with respect to natural gas supply depends not only on the low current price, but the expectation that prices will remain low into the future. The expectation of low and non-volatile prices for natural gas is not easy to relate to the historical price data shown in **Figure 3**. In the recent era of high prices, the assumption of many analysts was that prices were likely to remain high and increasing well into the future. This pessimistic conclusion was reached by considering the upward trend of consumption coupled with a declining resource base. Earlier, it was believed that natural gas was so abundant it could be treated as essentially a good with little value. These earlier failed expectations suggest that what appears to be a clear future path for natural gas markets can quickly reverse itself.

> Considerable uncertainty exists regarding the size of the economically recoverable U.S. shale gas resource base and the cost of producing those resources. Across four shale gas resource scenarios from the Annual Energy Outlook 2012 (AEO2012), natural gas prices vary by about $4 per million British thermal units (MMBtu) in 2035, demonstrating the significant impact that shale gas resource uncertainty has in determining future natural gas prices. This

---

[49] Environmental Protection Agency, http://yosemite.epa.gov/opei/RuleGate.nsf/.

uncertainty exists primarily because shale gas wells exhibit a wide variation in their initial production rate, rate of decline, and estimated ultimate recovery per well (or EUR, which is the expected cumulative production over the life of a well).[50]

Natural gas demand has not exhibited dramatic changes to correspond with its price volatility. For many of the final consuming sectors, households, commercial uses, and electric power generation the demand has been relatively price inelastic, insensitive to changes in price. This is because of the nature of natural gas use, primarily heating in households and commercial uses. Only in the industrial demand sector is there significant price elasticity as shown by the reductions in demand and plant closures associated with the last period of high prices.[51] The inelasticity of natural gas demand also means that relatively small variations in the quantity available can have surprisingly large effects on price. This is because, with inelastic demand, any shortage or surplus of supply requires a disproportionate variation in price to ration people out of or bring consumers into the market.

Price is also important to the potential expansion of the supply of natural gas. If prices fall, and remain, too low to provide an adequate return for producers, exploration and development will stagnate and future supply projections will prove to be optimistic. However, if the price of natural gas rises, and returns to producers rise, demand might be discouraged. The market must price natural gas in such a way that consumers are drawn to use more natural gas and that producers are encouraged to produce more natural gas. Consumers must also be incentivized to undertake the expense of changing fuels. Maintaining the status quo is a powerful force and overcoming it requires motivation beyond short-term gains because of prices. The market has not generated such razor-edged prices in the past.

Not only the price of natural gas will determine the state of the market. The price of oil and coal are also likely to play an important role. If the price gap between crude oil narrows, natural gas will become a less attractive source of energy than oil. The reason is likely to be habit and infrastructure. Consumers are used to using oil-based products and the infrastructure to supply them is well established. If the incentive of cost savings disappears, it is likely that the mass of consumers will continue using established products. Similarly, the cost of a new supply infrastructure is likely to be avoided if the anticipated demand growth of natural gas becomes more uncertain. For coal, electric power plants may be idled for some time while fuel prices give natural gas an advantage. But, if natural gas prices rise because of increased demand, coal may regain market share.

Demand Competition

Enthusiasm over the state of natural gas markets has led to plans of increased consumption in all demand categories. However, demand expansion differs among the EIA's demand segments. One characteristic that is common is that expanded demand only occurs after a lag. Low prices increase interest in expanding consumption, but then investments must take place before growth in consumption is realized. Once the investments are in place, which can take years, in many parts of the market it is hard to reverse them and go back to previously used fuels.

---

[50] U.S. Energy Information Administration, *Projected natural gas prices depend on shale gas resource economics*, August 27, 2012, http://www.eia.gov/todayinenergy/detail.cfm?id=7710#.

[51] See CRS Report R41628, *Industrial Demand and the Changing Natural Gas Market*, by Robert Pirog.

Expansion of household and commercial demand usually means natural gas for use in space heating. Conversion from other fuels is minimal, because of inadequate supply infrastructure, so the main source of new demand is new construction. Once a heating system in new construction is in place it is unlikely to be replaced by a different fuel. As a result, demand increases from these sectors are likely to be incremental and long-term.

Similarly, while the demand for natural gas in transportation is likely to exhibit sharp percentage increases relative to its small base, its overall effect on demand is likely to be incremental and permanent. Once vehicle conversions or vehicles with dedicated power plants are on the road and the natural gas supply infrastructure is in place, demand growth is likely to continue. After buying a home, a car is probably the next largest investment for most households and not likely to be changed because of short-term price changes.

Electric power generation and industrial use of natural gas are different. Much more rapid demand expansion can occur in these segments. Each consumer uses large quantities of gas and total demand can increase sharply. If the export of LNG expands, it would exhibit similar characteristics. Industrial demand is also likely to be price sensitive. Industrial demand has contracted in periods of high prices.

The combination of trend growth generated by household and commercial demand coupled with periodic large increases in demand associated with investment by power generators and industrial users could, if all planned expansions come to fruition, lead to a demand level which is too large relative to supply growth after the period of low prices. The result would likely be upward price volatility which could destabilize the market and reduce expected economic benefits.

Other Factors

Other legislative or regulatory policies could impact the natural gas market. For example, if legislation or regulation required tight carbon emission limits for electric power generators and the price of natural gas was low, a large increase in demand might be expected. Increases in demand from any source tend to raise prices. However, the price increases would tend to lead to increased development of natural gas resources and increased supply.

If offshore drilling opportunities were expanded, as oil and natural gas were discovered, domestic supplies would increase, causing the price of natural gas to fall. Falling prices would benefit consumers in the short-term, but would likely reduce the development of on-shore shale resources in the longer term, depending upon which sources had lower costs.

These two examples show that unintended consequences of policy decisions could affect natural gas markets. The results could upset the calculation of net economic benefits that the United States might expect to experience from development of the expanded shale gas resource base.

Conclusions

Given existing data, most indications point to the changes in the natural gas industry as positive to the overall U.S. economy. Industries that use natural gas as an input have seen prices fall. Producers have expanded the U.S. resource base tremendously, including for oil. Low prices have forced producers to be innovative and drive down production costs. Similarly, environmental concerns are prompting companies to be more proactive in addressing these issues. Also responding to environmental concerns, a number of major natural gas and oil producing states have revised their rules, which has not appeared to have inhibited production in those states.

The next five years will be telling as proposed projects will either come to fruition, be postponed, or be cancelled. Investment decisions are being made given existing realities and future perceptions of the market. Many of the environmental concerns may be addressed by industry, federal, state, and local governments, and the market. Production efficiencies and extraction improvements, particularly in regards to water use, are likely to be made in this time period.

Congress may act on a variety of issues that would affect natural gas. Legislation has been introduced that could increase the supply of natural gas by opening up more federal lands and offshore areas to exploration, by providing direct incentives for natural gas production, and by limiting federal regulations on federal lands. Other legislation may inhibit natural gas production by eliminating incentives, increasing regulatory requirements on companies, or limiting access to potential areas of development. Legislation has also been introduced that could increase demand for natural gas by vehicles and in aviation. Although some Members have expressed support for LNG exports, legislation has been introduced that would delay LNG exports, thereby limiting a potential source of demand. Still other legislation has been introduced that would promote natural gas infrastructure in some areas and other legislation has been introduced to limit the environmental effects of natural gas production. Similarly, rules and regulations are being proposed at different federal agencies, for example the Departments of Energy and Interior, and the Environmental Protection Agency, which may require or elicit congressional input.

Appendix A.

Figure A-1. U.S. Natural Gas Infrastructure and Shale Resources

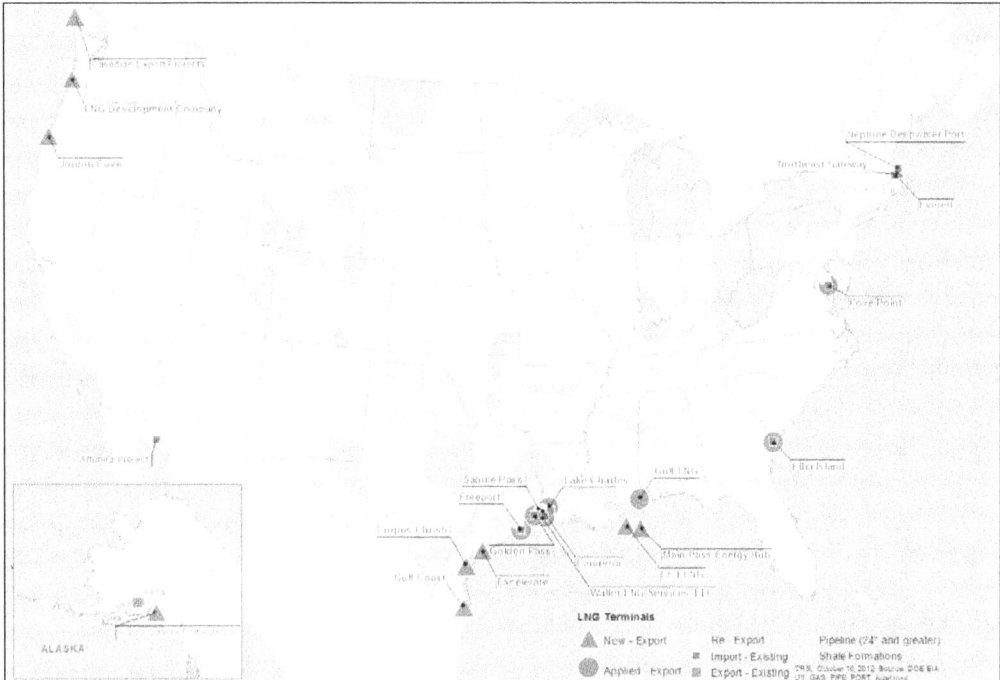

Source: Compiled by CRS using data from the Department of Energy and the U.S. Energy Information Administration.

Appendix B.

Figure B-1. State Production and Consumption, 2011
% of total U.S. production and consumption

Source: U.S. Energy Information Administration, http://www.eia.gov/dnav/ng/ng_prod_sum_dcu_NUS_a.htm and http://www.eia.gov/dnav/ng/ng_cons_sum_dcu_nus_a.htm.

Notes: Production is dry gas production.

Appendix C.

Table C-1. Energy Conversions and Comparisons

Fuel	Unit	Btu Equivalent
Natural Gas	1 cubic foot	1,032 Btu
Gasoline	1 gallon	124,238 Btu
Diesel	1 gallon	138,690 Btu
Coal	1 short ton	19,858,000 Btu
Electricity	1 kilowatthour	3,412 Btu

Source: U.S. Energy Information Administration, http://www.eia.gov/energyexplained/index.cfm?page=about_energy_units.

Notes: Btu = British thermal unit.

Author Contact Information

Robert Pirog
Specialist in Energy Economics
rpirog@crs.loc.gov, 7-6847

Michael Ratner
Specialist in Energy Policy
mratner@crs.loc.gov, 7-9529

Acknowledgments

James Uzel and Amber Wilhelm contributed to the graphics of this report.